686

PEOPLE AT WORK

MAKING BOOKS

Deborah Fox

Evans

EVANS BROTHERS LIMITED

Published by Evans Brothers Limited
2a Portman Mansions
Chiltern Street
London
W1M 1LE

© 2000 Evans Brothers Limited

First published in 2000

All rights reserved. No part of this publication may be reproduced, stored in a retrieval system or transmitted in any form or by any means, electronic, mechanical, photocopying, recording or otherwise, without prior permission of Evans Brothers Limited.

Commissioned by: Su Swallow
Design: Neil Sayer
Photography: Gareth Boden; Peter Millard; Alan Towse
Illustrator: Liam Bonney/The Art Market

British Library Cataloguing in Publication Data

Fox, Deborah
  People at work making books
  1.Printers - Juvenile literature 2.Book design - Juvenile literature
  I.Title II.Making books
  686

ISBN 0237519666

Printed in Hong Kong by Wing King Tong

Acknowledgements

The author and publisher wish to thank the following for their help:
Mary Tapissier, Kate Burns, Linda Nelson and all the staff at Hodder Children's Books; Phil Smith of Dot Gradations, Wickford, Essex, and John Grove and Hilary Panting of Ebenezer Baylis, Worcester.

Our thanks also to Cressida Cowell, the author and illustrator of *Little Bo-Peep's Library* published by Hodder Children's Books.

All photographs by Gareth Boden except for pages 11, 12, 13 (top) and 27 by Peter Millard and pages 22 (bottom), 23, 24 and 25 by Alan Towse.

Contents

The ideas	8
Working out the costs	10
The pictures	12
Editing the words and pictures	14
Designing the cover	16
Making colour proofs	18
Printing colour proofs	20
At the printer's	22
The finished books	24
Making more books	26
Glossary	28
Index	29

The ideas

I'm Kate and I work in children's book publishing. I'm a picture-book publisher. I think up new ideas for picture books for our publishing company. There are three other publishers here – one for story books, one for non-fiction and one for our books on tape.

Thinking up ideas

Last year 8497 books were published in this country. There are a lot of children's book publishers, all competing to publish the most popular books. Our company publishes over 300 new books a year. Every two weeks I meet with the other publishers and editors to discuss our new ideas. Last week I was very excited when I met a new illustrator. I'd like to work with her on a new picture book.

▶ Publishers and editors meet every two weeks to discuss new ideas.

▲ I'd like to use a new illustrator for one of our picture books and so I take two of her pictures to our acquisitions meeting.

Selling the ideas

One week after our editorial meeting, we each present our best ideas to the managing director and other people in the company. This meeting is known as the 'acquisitions meeting' because it is where we acquire, or take on, new titles. It's important to be really enthusiastic about our ideas because that helps our sales people to sell the books to customers in this country and all over the world.

> I work on about 30 new books a year, mainly for the under fives. I really enjoy getting a new picture-book story from an author and thinking, "Now which illustrator will bring out the best in this?"

Working out the costs

Some books cost more than others to make. A story book with no pictures is cheaper than a colour book with pictures on every page. When we take our new ideas to the meeting we must know how much the book will cost to make. Our production department works out the total costs. We tell them how many pages the book will have, what size it will be, whether there are illustrations and if so how many, whether there are any novelty bits in the book like pop-ups or flaps, and how much we will have to pay the author and the illustrator. The production team then put all the figures in to their computers.

◀ I talk to our production director about a new idea. She has ordered a blank copy of the book from the printer. It has no words or pictures in it at all and is called a 'dummy'. It is useful to show the people who sell our books what size and shape the new book will be.

The author Cressida Cowell writes her picture-book stories by hand. Because she illustrates too, she likes to make her own little book of the story, showing her sketches and the words.

Too expensive?

Colour books cost more to make than black-and-white books. Our sales director tells us how many copies of each book he thinks he can sell. We need to sell enough copies to cover all the costs of making the book, including paying the author and illustrator, plus some extra so that our company makes a profit. Our accounts people look very carefully at the figures to make sure we've got the right balance between spending money and selling enough books.

Saying yes

If everyone likes the new idea, we tell the author and the illustrator that we can go ahead. We agree when the text and pictures should be sent to me.

Writing

Some of my authors write the words, or text, by hand and never use a computer. Other authors always use a computer. For books with a lot of words, we prefer to have the text on disk because we don't want to type it all up.

The pictures

Pictures bring stories to life. An important part of my job is matching an illustrator with a story. It's no good choosing a 'cartoony' style of illustration for a sad story. The illustrator reads a copy of the text and then draws some sketches which we call 'roughs'. The illustrators know how many pages the book has and how many pictures there should be. When they send their roughs to me, I always send a copy to the author. If the author and I have any comments or suggestions, we discuss them with the illustrator.

Own styles

Each illustrator has his or her own style of illustration – some prefer to draw funny pictures, others like drawing animals and some like drawing people. When I meet new illustrators, they bring in some examples of their work.

> I use a pen and ink to create thick, squidgy outlines and I love the washy, splodgy effect you get from watercolours.
>
> Cressida, illustrator

◀ Cressida, who writes and illustrates, often draws each illustration seven or eight times before she is happy with the result.

◀ Cressida uses a pen and ink to create the lines around the people and objects in her pictures. She uses watercolours when she paints.

Illustrating
- A piece of artwork covering two pages of a book could take an artist two weeks to paint.
- An artist might need up to a year to complete the artwork for a book with 32 pages.

Designing the book

The designer's job is to make the text and pictures fit together and look good on the page. Before computers, designers used to stick pieces of text on paper, which took quite a long time! If there were any changes, they had to do the whole thing again ... just like using the 'cut and paste' on a computer today! Computers have made the job of the designer much easier. When designers get the illustrations, they can put them in to the computer using a machine called a scanner.

▲ After the designer has scanned in the illustrations, he moves them into the correct position on the computer screen.

Editing the words and pictures

Although designers look after the pictures and the editors look after the words, their jobs often do overlap. Editors check the text carefully to make sure that it reads well, it is the right length and that there are no spelling mistakes. They also look closely at the pictures to make sure that they work with the words.

Each book has its own schedule, stating when every stage of making the book should be done. The editors and the production team have

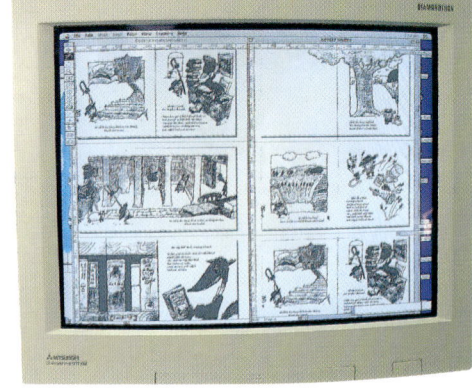

▲ The words and pictures together.

▼ The designer and editor often have meetings to look through the 'layouts' of a book, showing the text and pictures on a page.

regular meetings to discuss the schedules and to report if there are any problems that might make the books late.

Choosing a typeface

When the editor has edited the text, the text goes to the designer. The designers choose a typeface, which is the style of the lettering, and a type size for each book. They think about what age group the book is aimed at, how many words there are on the page and what sort of typeface suits the topic of the book.

Typefaces

- There are thousands of typefaces today, each with their own name, such as ALPHABET SOUP TILT, **American typewriter**, Arnold Bocklin and Formal Script 421.
- The size of the type on the printed page is known as the 'point' size, So this small type is 6 point and this larger type is 24 point.

Photographs

Some books are illustrated with photographs. The author or editor writes a list of all the photos they want in the book. Many publishing companies have picture researchers who find the photographs. The picture researchers go to picture libraries because they have thousands of photographs from all over the world. The library sends a selection of photos to the picture researcher. The editor, author and picture researcher then have a meeting to choose the best. Sometimes it is better to hire a photographer to take the photos for a book – we did that for this book!

▼ *The picture researcher looks at the photographs sent to her by a picture library.*

Designing the cover

> When I work with illustrators, I'm always amazed at how clever, creative and talented they are. They often design the picture books themselves. They have worked out the whole thing.
>
> Claire, art director

▲ When the illustrator sends in the piece of artwork for the front cover, the designer scans it in to the computer.

The cover of a book is so important because it is the first thing customers see. If people don't like the cover, they might not open the book. Our art director, who is the head of the design team, sends all the cover designs to our sales people for their opinions and comments. A comment like "I don't like blue," isn't very helpful for the designer, but if someone gives a reason, such as "Blue won't work for this title because it looks too dark and

▶ The designer experiments with the green background on the picture. Should it be lighter? Working on computer means the designer can change colours quite easily.

16

won't stand out from a distance", the designer then understands why a change needs to be made.

Designers want the cover to tell the reader what the book is about and so they need to decide what picture they should show on the front, what the lettering should look like, how big it should be and what colours they should use. The cover will be used by the sales and publicity people in their catalogues, on leaflets and on the internet. It has to be eye-catching and well designed.

> When I'm designing story book covers, the editor gives me a 'brief' telling me what the story is about, because I don't have time to read all the books we publish. Sometimes the editor might suggest a picture for the cover, and sometimes I talk to illustrators about my ideas.
>
> Clare, art director

▼ The designer is ready to choose the style of lettering for the front cover. The illustrator has left space for the title of the book and the author's name.

Making colour proofs

▲ The four printing colours.

▶ Scanning the illustrations. The operator wraps an illustration around the drum. She keys in the size the picture will be on the printed page.

When the editor is sure that the text is correct and everything is in the right place, then the designer can pass the text on disk and all the illustrations to the production team. Its job is to get the book printed. The next thing I will see are the colour proofs, which are pages that show what the pictures and text look like on paper.

Four colours

How many colours are in a picture – ten, twenty, a hundred? The colour-proofing company separates the thousands of colours in illustrations and photographs into the four colours that can be printed – red (magenta), blue (cyan), yellow and black. From

18

these four it is possible to make all other colours. To split an artist's illustrations into the four colours, the proofers use a scanner. They wrap each illustration around a drum. As it spins round, a lens reads, or scans, all the colours and separates them into the printing colours.

Working on computer

After all the illustrations have been scanned, the proofers call up the scans on their computer screens to check that nothing is missing. They can now do detailed work on the pages of the book, like changing or adding colours. When they are happy that all the pages of the book are ready for colour-proofing, the pages (on disk) are printed out as pieces of film.

Colour proofs

- It takes five minutes to scan an A4-size piece of artwork at the same size. If the picture needs to be bigger, then it takes longer.
- Illustrators paint on flexible board because each illustration is wrapped around a drum.

From film to plate

There are four pieces of film for each page of the book – one piece for each of the colours. But to be able to print the proofs, the proofers have to use printing plates – one for each colour. To transfer the images on the film to the printing plates, they use a large camera.

◁ Arthur gets the film ready for the camera. Here he sticks down 16 pages of red film. The position of the pages is carefully worked out. It takes him about two hours to prepare the film for all four colours. Each piece of film is then taken to the camera.

Printing colour proofs

◀ Printing the colour proofs. You can see that two colours have been printed – the yellow and the blue.

▼ All the colours have been printed. The operator checks the quality of the colours with an eye-glass. You can see one of the metal printing plates on the machine.

▶ *There is a colour bar along the edge of the colour proofs. The machine checks the strength of each colour. If the colours aren't just right, the proofers print a new proof.*

The metal printing plates are loaded on to the printing machine. There is a separate plate for each of the four colours – red, yellow, blue and black. The colours are printed one at a time. Gradually the colours build up until the proofs look just like the original illustrations. On each side of a large sheet of paper there are usually 16 pages of the book, but there can be more or less. The position of each page is carefully planned because all the pages must be in the right order when the sheet of paper is folded.

Checking colour proofs

Production check the colour proofs carefully to make sure the colours on the proofs match the artist's illustrations, or the photographs. If one of the colours is too strong, it can affect the balance of colour. Production will then ask for a new or 'revised' proof to re-check the colour before we print the book.

◀ *The production manager checks the colour proofs against the artist's illustrations. I like to see them too.*

21

At the printer's

The next stage is to print the book. The colour-proofing company sends all the film to the printer's. The printer makes sure that all the pages of the book are in the right order and sends us a final set of proofs, called 'ozalids'. This is our last chance to correct anything that is wrong.

The printing plates

As soon as we have checked the ozalids, the printer makes the printing plates for the four printing colours, just as the colour-proofers did. Often there are 16 pages on one plate. The printer prints on both sides of the

▲ Our production director checks the ozalid proofs against the colour proofs, making sure all the pages are in the right order.

▶ The images from one of the colour films have been transferred on to the metal printing plate by the camera.

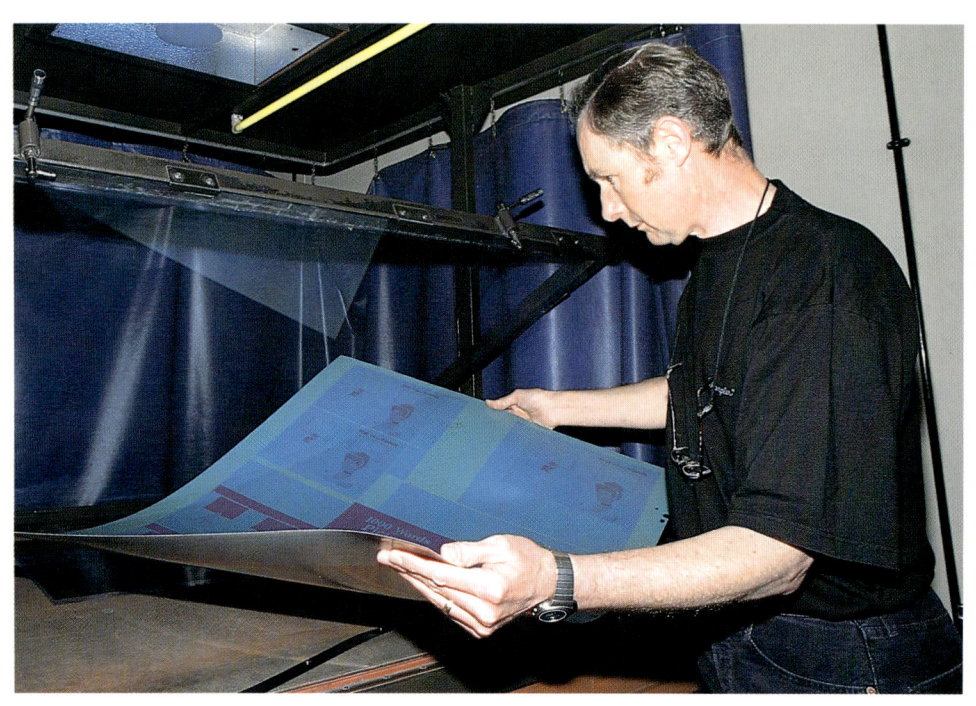

▲ Before the book is printed, the operator loads all the plates on the printing machine and checks that they are in position.

▼ The operator spreads out the red ink in the ink duct. He can top up the ink during printing.

paper, which makes a 32-page book or a 32-page 'section' of a longer book.

The printing press

Getting a printing machine ready to print all the pages in a book takes about an hour. The operators have to fill the ducts with ink, they need to load the metal printing plates on to the machine and get the paper ready. The operators run some paper through the machine until they are sure that the ink is running smoothly and that all the pages are in focus. If one of the plates is slightly out of position, the printed pages will look fuzzy.

Printing
- The four-colour printing machine costs about £1,000,000.
- The operators waste about 50 sheets of paper for each new printing checking that the colour is running smoothly.

23

The finished books

When the pages have been printed, they have to be folded and then bound together to make a book. The printed sheets go to a folding machine and then through to a binding machine, where the different sections of the book are either stitched, glued or stapled together.

Binding the books

The sections of the book travel along the binding machine and drop on top of each other in the right order. Then they

▲ The operator pulls out a printed sheet to check the quality. When each sheet is folded, the pages will be in the right order.

Binding a book

- The glue that is used to stick the book together is heated to a temperature of 150°C. It sets in about a minute.
- The folding machine folds about 12,500 sheets of paper an hour.
- Hardback books have a 'spine'.

▲ The folding machine. Two people collect the folded 'sections' as they come off the machine.

24

◀ We are thrilled when we see the printed books for the first time.

▼ Every book is trimmed. This creates a lot of waste paper. The printer collects the waste, packs it into bales and sends it off for recycling. They get £1 for each bale.

are either stitched together and glued, stapled, or just glued together. The sections then move along to the trimming machine, which shaves off the three edges of the books (not the spine as this has been glued!). All the waste bits of paper are collected and sent for recycling.

Book have either hard or soft covers. A hardback cover is wrapped around a hard piece of board, which is then wrapped around the book by the binding machine.

To the warehouse

When the printed books have gone through all the stages – folding, binding and trimming – staff pack them up in boxes and send them to our warehouse.

Making more books

Long before the books reach the warehouse, our publicity and marketing staff have been thinking of ways to get our new books noticed. They might get posters or badges designed and printed, or a soft-toy version made of one of the characters in our books. They send out free books to newspapers and magazines to try to get them reviewed, and they ask our authors and illustrators to talk to schools and bookshops.

▶ Our rights manager, who sells the books to other countries, her assistant and the art director, who is in charge of design, discuss what to include in a leaflet that will be sent to our foreign customers.

Selling abroad

As it is so expensive to make colour books, we try to sell them to other countries, who translate them into their own languages. Our rights manager travels abroad to show our books to foreign publishers.

Books on tape

You don't always have to read books, you can listen to them too! Our publishing director is responsible for turning some of our best-selling books into audio books, recorded on cassette-tape. She has to book a studio where the actors and actresses can record their characters' voices. Sometimes just one actor reads the whole book.

▼ Sales representatives sell our books to bookshops throughout the country. Other representatives visit schools.

◀ Recording one of our audio books. The producer at the studio has hired the actors and actresses for the day. The script has been approved by our publishing director.

It can take two years before one of my books is published. I commission some busy authors and illustrators three years in advance.

Glossary

artwork the illustrations (pictures)

author the person who writes the book

commission to ask an author or illustrator to write or illustrate a book

dummy a book with a blank cover and blank pages

editor the person in charge of putting a book together

layouts the arrangement of text and pictures on a page

marketing using advertisements and other publicity to help sell things

novelty books books that have unusual features like pop-up pages, lift the flaps, or moving parts

picture books books with lots of pictures for very young children

publicity advertising, reviews and other materials that draw attention to a product; the department that is in charge of publicity

publisher the company responsible for making books; a publisher is also the person responsible for thinking of new books and finding authors and illustrators for them

sales representatives the people who travel to shops or organisations in order to sell their company's product

schedule a list of the dates by which different stages of the book should be completed

section a sheet of paper that has been printed and folded to create pages in a book

soft cover describes a book that has a thin cover; a paperback

spine the narrow central part of a book's cover, showing the title and author, which is usually face out on a bookshelf

text the words of a book

typeface the style or design of letters or words

Index

acquisitions meeting 9
art director 16, 17, 26
artist 13, 19, 21
artwork 13, 16, 19, 28
audio books 27
author 10, 11, 12, 15, 26, 28

badges 26
binding machine 24, 25
black-and-white books 11
bookshops 26, 27

catalogues 17
colour books 10, 11
colour proofs 18, 19, 20, 21
computers 10, 11, 13, 16, 19
costs 10-11, 27
covers 16, 17, 25

designer 13, 14, 15, 16, 17
design team 16
dummy 10, 28

editorial meeting 9
editors 8, 14, 15, 17, 18, 28

folding paper 24, 25
foreign customers 9, 26, 27

ideas 8, 9, 10, 27
illustration styles 12
illustrator 8, 9, 10, 11, 12, 16, 17, 19, 26, 28
internet 17

layouts 14, 28
leaflets 17, 26

magazine reviews 26, 28
managing director 9
marketing 26, 28

newspaper reviews 26, 28
non-fiction books 8
novelty books 10, 28

ozalids 22, 28

pages of book 10, 12, 21, 22, 23, 24, 28
paper 23, 25, 28
photographs 15, 21
picture books 8, 9, 11, 28
picture libraries 15
picture researchers 15
pop-ups 10, 28
posters 26
printer 22
printing plates 19, 21, 22, 23
production department 10, 14, 18, 21

production director 10, 22
publicity 17, 26, 28
publishers 8, 28

recycling paper 25
reviews 26
revised proofs 21
rights manager 26, 27
roughs 12

sales 9, 16, 17, 26, 27
sales director 11
scanning 13, 16, 17, 18, 19
schedules 14, 15, 28
schools 26, 27
selling books 9, 10, 11, 26, 27, 28
sketches 11, 12
spelling 14
stories 12
story books 8, 9, 10, 17

tape (books on) 8, 27
text 11, 12, 13, 14, 18, 28
typeface 15, 28
type size 15

warehouse 25, 26
watercolours 12, 13
words 10, 11, 14, 15, 28